A folk fable

Richard Lessor

Argus Communications
7440 Natchez Avenue
Niles, Illinois 60648

International Standard Book Number: 0-913592-60-9
Library of Congress Number: 75-24587

6   7   8   9   0

To my son, Bill,
and to Warren and Doug—
lives lived in awareness
that to restrict another's growth
is to self-destruct.
Don't hoard Your Fuzzies!

Come with us
to the make-believe Valley of Fuzzies.
You will experience
the pristine beauty
of a land of love and happiness.
Learn the secret
shared only by valley people.
Relive with them
the halcyon days of yore,
those unforgettable days of joy
until . . . .
Well, you'll have to read it
for yourself to believe it.

Once upon a time,
not so long ago
as you might suspect,
there was a beautiful valley
which was surrounded by mountains
and just far enough
from the Interstate Expressway
to make it impossible
for tourists to reach.

Vacationers would look
at the map and see
that none of the roads
which led there
was printed in the nice bold, red lines
which they liked to see.
They thought about bumps
and unimproved shoulders
and dust coming in
through the tailgates
of their station wagons,
and they drove right on by the exit
which would have taken them
to the valley.

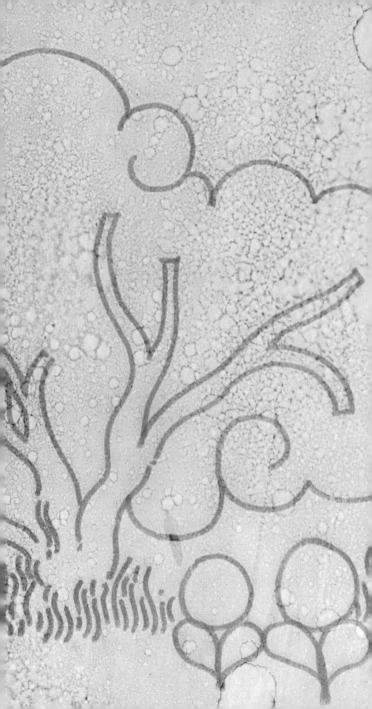

From the big highway
the mountains in the distance
seemed like a steep wall,
and there was no sign
of the rich green valley
which these walls surrounded.
So for years
hundreds of thousands of cars
just whizzed by.
They were wise to do so,
because,
since nobody ever went to the valley,
there were no motels,
no gas stations,
no drive-ins,
not even a miniature golf course
along the way.
Nothing but scenery
as a matter of fact.

And, if you can imagine
anything so pitiful,
the people of the valley
were so simple
that they didn't even know
what they were missing.
They just kept right on living,
and working,
and loving there

without ever tasting a Dairy Delight
or getting caught in a traffic jam.
They were very ordinary people indeed,
just like you'd find
anywhere else,
except for two things:
They were happy.
They had Fuzzies.

13

Now a lot of people
are happy sometimes—
at parties,
or when they get a new television set,
or win a contest—
but the valley people
were happy
almost all of the time.
They were happy on Monday mornings;
they were happy when it rained;
they were happy when the children
had a free day from school
in the middle of the week;
they were even happy at work.
They were simple people
as we've seen.
So simple
that they didn't even know
that it takes things
to make you happy
or that other people
could make you unhappy.

Their problem was
that they liked people.
They didn't even know enough
to mistrust them,
or be suspicious.
For instance,
people in the valley
never locked their doors
or thought about counting their change.

They even enjoyed talking
to one another
and would go out of their way
to do each other favors.
Most of all,
they enjoyed meeting
and greeting each other.

This should be blamed
on the Fuzzies,
of course.
Early in the history of the valley
the first settlers
discovered these small,
roly-poly little creatures
who sat up
on their plump little haunches
and regarded them cheerfully
from between the stems of flowers
or around the end of a fallen branch.
They were like little puffs of soft fur—
perfectly round,
warm and soft.

18

They made absolutely no effort
to run away,
and in fact
what they liked most
was being picked up and held.
Their fur was so soft,
and they felt so good in the hand
that the settlers named them Fuzzies.
They were small and cuddly and soft—
and looked at you
with such absolute trust
as they curled up in your hand
that the people never dreamed
of eating one,
even if they had to go to bed
without any supper.
In fact, if you were hungry
or tired or worried,
just picking up a Fuzzy
somehow made you feel better.

20

Aside from an occasional owl
or greedy chicken hawk,
the Fuzzies had no natural enemies
in the valley,
and they prospered
and multiplied quite rapidly.
But as the population
of the valley grew
the settlers began to catch the Fuzzies
and keep them
in little pens behind their houses—
because once you picked a Fuzzy up
you hated to put him down,

and the thought
of letting him out of your sight again
was hard to bear.
They were no trouble to keep—
just a handful of corn
or wheat or even bread crumbs
would keep them fat and healthy.
Gradually so many Fuzzies
were picked up and kept
that none remained to be found
in the woods or garden.

23

And the people began
to miss the joy
of finding a new Fuzzy
to add to their collection—
for as much alike as every Fuzzy looked,
each one was somehow different,
and seemed just right
for whomever was holding him
for the first time.

So the custom
of exchanging Fuzzies
grew over many years.
At first
people gave them
to young people getting married
and setting up a new household.
Then they started
taking them to sick people
to cheer them up.

Every young child
was given some Fuzzies
of his very own.
Finally it got to the point
where people
couldn't bear to be without them
too many "times"
and carried them about
in a special Fuzzy bag
so that they could exchange them
at any time during the day.
And, strangely enough,
Fuzzies gave them something
to look forward to.
They looked forward
to meeting each other
and going places,
because you could never tell
who might give you a Fuzzy.

So, simple that they were,
they enjoyed each day as it came
and hardly knew how to be bored
or tired of seeing the same old faces
and going to the same old places.
You do really have to be simple
not to enjoy smoking
or drinking
or taking pills
to make you feel better;
so simple
that a silly little thing
like exchanging Fuzzies
and just living
keeps you happy.

That's just what the head witch
in charge of the Blahs thought
when she accidentally
happened to see
the awful situation
which existed
in the valley of the Fuzzies
as she flew over
on her jet broom.

34

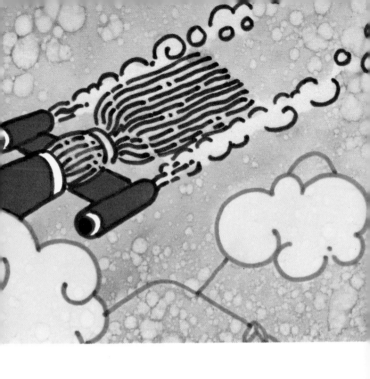

"This is ridiculous,"
she said out loud.
"I've got to do something
for those poor people.
They're so simple
that they may spend
their whole lives
thinking they are happy
when they can't possibly know
what it means."

You don't get to be head witch
just by riding around
on a jet broomstick
or putting razor blades
in apples on Halloween.
You've got to work
at being cagey
and nasty
all year round.
You can't come on too strong,
either,
or most people will think
you're part of a promotional campaign
to sell margarine
or detergents
and not pay any attention to you.

And this particular witch,
whose name was Juanita,
was one of the best in the business.

She cast a spell or two
and whipped up
an evil-smelling potion
just for old times' sake,
but then she went to the library
and looked at some history books.

It didn't take her long
to come up with a fool-proof plan
to help the people in the valley
get rid of the dangerous
and foolish notion
that they were happy.

On the first available
Friday the thirteenth
she changed her jet broom
into a red sports helicopter
and crossed the precipitous ridge
into the green valley.
When she got there
she stopped in front of
the first little white cottage she saw
and pretended
her motor was overheated.

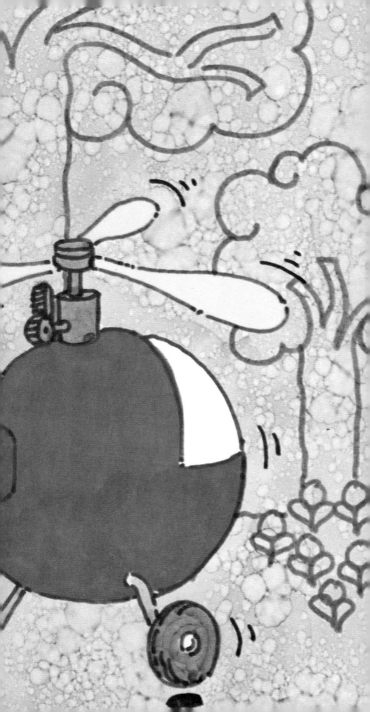

In a matter of seconds
the woman who lived in the cottage
came running to the window
to see what was causing
all the racket.
She was amazed
to see a woman
climb out of the noisy red bird.
Frightened though she was
by the big bird with its whirly wings
she timidly opened her door
with a Fuzzy in her hand
to greet this unusual guest.

Juanita,
who was wearing a mini-skirt
and a hot pink blouse,
took the Fuzzy in her hand
and squeezed it so tightly
that it squealed
and squirmed out of her fingers.

"Oh dear,"
said the woman,
"I'm so sorry.
That's the first time
I've ever seen a Fuzzy run away.
Perhaps it is afraid
of your big red bird.
But don't worry.
I'll give you another one."

They went inside
for a cup of tea,
and Juanita admired
all the woman's furniture and china
and asked about her family.
The woman was so cheerful
and friendly and happy
that it almost made Juanita
choke on her tea.
But if her plan was to work,
she'd have to stand it
a while longer.

Finally the woman asked
what the witch
had been waiting to hear.
"Would you like to see our Fuzzies?
We don't like to brag
or seem to show-off,
but we think
we have some of the finest
in the valley."

She took Juanita out into the garden
and showed her the tiny pen
where the Fuzzies
were rolling and tumbling and playing.

"How many do you have?"
said Juanita,
pretending that she was fascinated
with the disgustingly
happy little creatures.

47

"Well," said the woman
counting on her fingers,
"subtracting the one that just ran away
and the three
that my husband gave away yesterday,
we should have twenty-four."

"Yesterday when your husband
gave the Fuzzies away,
didn't he get any in return?"
Juanita asked innocently.

"Goodness, no!"
the woman replied.
"Yesterday we went to a christening,
a bar mitzvah, and a wedding.
You only give Fuzzies
on such occasions;
you don't expect one in return."

"It's none of my business,"
said Juanita slyly,
"but it sounds like
you're in trouble to me.
If you keep on at that rate
you'll be out of Fuzzies
in another week or so.
Did it ever occur to you
that people
may deliberately be inviting you places
just to get your Fuzzies
away from you?"

"But why
would anyone want to do that?"
cried the woman,
who for about the first time
in her life
felt a strange
sinking feeling in her stomach
and the traces of an ache
at the base of her head.

"Oh," said Juanita
ever so casually
as she walked
toward her red copter,
"Haven't you heard
about the terrible shortage
of Fuzzies?"

"Good heavens!"
said the woman,
forgetting her manners
and not even remembering
to say goodbye.
Juanita watched her
in the rear-view mirror
as she flew away.
The woman was down
on her hands and knees
in the front yard
looking for the Fuzzy
that had run away.

Now it was Juanita's turn
to be happy.
Her plan was going to work.

If she could have remembered how,
she would have laughed
out loud.
And her plan did work.
The woman told her husband
what Juanita had said.
He stopped giving
and exchanging Fuzzies,
and pretty soon
people began to notice
that he was taking and not giving.

So they stopped giving too,
and worried about
running out of Fuzzies
themselves.

It didn't take long
before everyone realized
that there was a serious
shortage of Fuzzies.

People started
crossing to the other side
of the street
so they wouldn't be expected
to exchange Fuzzies.

They stopped visiting each other.
When they did have to go
to a wedding
or a birthday party
they gave money or gift certificates.

With nowhere much to go
and not many people to talk to,
people became restless and bored.
Mostly they just sat around
and worried
that something might happen
to their Fuzzies.

And, sure enough,
one day
a dozen families awoke
to find that their Fuzzies
had been stolen during the night.

They got together
and appointed a sheriff
and organized a vigilante committee
to patrol the streets after dark.

59

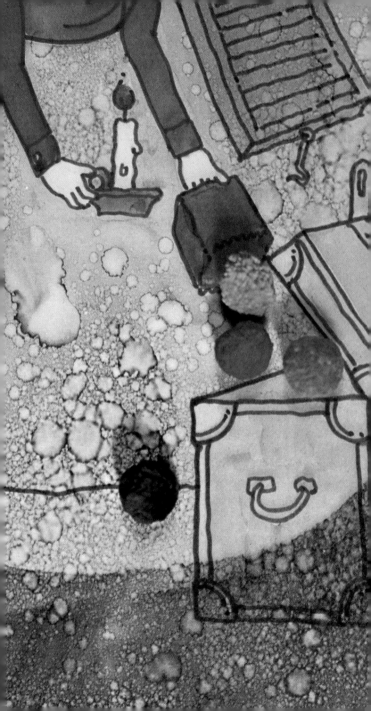

People brought their Fuzzies
in from the outdoor pens
and locked them away
in dark cupboards and basements
where the little creatures languished
without fresh air and sunlight.

Their coats
grew dull and matted,
and they no longer
sat on their haunches
or begged to be picked up.
Eventually, of course,
many of them simply died.
The cloudless Fuzzy days
turned into
Fuzziless cloudy days.

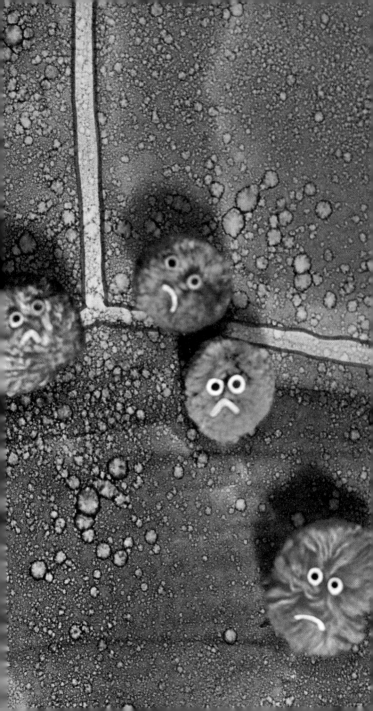

The Fuzziless months
turned into Fuzziless years,
and soon there were
a few young people in the valley
who had actually
never seen a Fuzzy,
much less exchanged or owned one.

One man who died
willed all his Fuzzies to his son,
but when the young man
went to collect them
he was so disgusted
by the sight of the
sickly, skinny, mouse-like animals
he found in a secret room
in his father's attic
that he picked up the pen
and threw it out the window.

Eventually the people in the valley decided to cross the mountain to see if things were better on the other side.

After that,
their young people
began leaving
to work in cities,
since there was very little
to do in the valley.

They sent a delegation
to the governor
to demand
that a six-lane road be built
to connect with the Interstate,
and he agreed.

Soon progress came to the valley
along with lots of tourists,
billboards,
housing projects,
parking lots,
and even a drive-in movie.

And the people of the valley
were busier
than ever before in their lives.
But not happier.

No one bothered
with Fuzzies anymore.
In fact, nobody remembered
what it was
they'd ever seen in them.

No one, that is,
but the woman who'd been visited
by Juanita the witch.

One day
she was telling her grandchildren
a story about the valley
in the olden days—
about how you could cross the street
without going over a traffic bridge
and how you could
actually swim in the lake.

She also told the children
about the Fuzzies
and what happiness it had been
to exchange them
and to hold them.
The children all got excited
about the Fuzzies
and wanted to know
if they could see one on television
or in a zoo.
But as the woman
leaned back and laughed
a piercing thought
came to her:
"I wonder what life
would have been like
if there hadn't been a shortage
of Fuzzies?"